Unlocking the Beauty of
The Catechism

The Creed: Part One
Facilitator's Guide

Christopher J. Ruff, S.T.L.

Unlocking the Beauty of the Catechism
The Creed: Part One – Facilitator's Guide

Novo Millennio Press
PO Box 160
La Crescent, MN 55947
www.novomill.com

Nihil obstat: Rev. Jesse D. Burish, S.T.L.
Censor Librorum

Imprimatur: William Patrick Callahan, OFM Conv.
Bishop of La Crosse
August 15, 2012

The *nihil obstat* and *imprimatur* are official declarations that a book or pamphlet is free of doctrinal or moral error. No implication is contained therein that those who have granted the *nihil obstat* and *imprimatur* agree with the contents, opinions, or statements expressed.

Cover art:
Manuel Panselinos, *Christ Enthroned.*
Protaton church, Mount Athos, Greece, ca 1290.
Image compliments of skete.com.

Graphics and Design:
Alice J. Andersen
www.alicejandersen.com.

Introduction

The Facilitator's Role

Welcome to the Facilitator's Guide for *Unlocking the Beauty of the Catechism – Part One: The Creed.*

Perhaps you are your group's designated facilitator throughout this course of shared study. Or perhaps your group has decided its members will take turns acting as the facilitator, and it is now your turn. Either way, the facilitator's role is a humble but important one.

Let me emphasize one thing right away. You are not expected to have any more wisdom or knowledge about the *Catechism of the Catholic Church* than any other member of the group. The Catechism itself is the teacher, supplemented by the study guide *(Unlocking the Beauty of the Catechism)*. Your primary role, as stated in the study guide itself, is "to start and end the meeting on time, to help keep things moving and on topic, and to foster a friendly, supportive environment in which everyone feels invited to contribute."

The rest of your role can easily be seen in the following excerpt from "Keys to a Successful Catechism Study," taken from the study guide itself.

Conducting the Session

1. The facilitator calls the gathering to order and all pray together the opening prayer.

2. The group participants then take turns reading aloud the study guide material for that session (one or two paragraphs at a time—whatever seems reasonable). This rotating pattern should continue through the discussion questions.

   - **NOTE:** Consistent feedback has confirmed that this practice of reading aloud the study guide material enhances the group experience, even though participants have already read it on their own. Starting with the opening prayer, it typically takes only 10-15 minutes to arrive at the first discussion question.

3. If a discussion question asks for some passages of Scripture to be read, this should also be done aloud if time permits, though it is presumed that people have done this on their own in preparation for the meeting.

4. The facilitator has a Facilitator's Guide with "answer prompts" for some questions, and this may be helpful if the discussion stalls or there is confusion. But the guide should be used sparingly or it will get in the way of genuine discussion. The group should try to answer every question as thoroughly as possible before there is any consultation of the Facilitator's Guide.

5. If in the course of the discussion there arises a question or controversy that cannot be resolved in the group, the facilitator should consult the pastor or another resource person with a solid theological formation between sessions, bringing their response back to the group.

6. When there are 10-15 minutes left in the allotted schedule for the meeting, the facilitator should note that it is time to draw the discussion to a close (even if some discussion questions remain) and to move on to reading the brief "Growth in Discipleship" section, and praying the "Group Prayers of Intercession."

7. The purpose of the "Growth in Discipleship" section is to provide ideas for personal application. These can be discussed if people wish, but there is no need for any commitments to be made publicly, unless people want to plan, for example, to pray the rosary together, or carry out some work of service, etc.

8. The "Group Prayers of Intercession" are intended to be spontaneous prayer intentions. They direct the power of prayer to various needs and simultaneously deepen the spirit of fellowship in the group. Conclude with the Lord's Prayer.

9. The session should end on time, even if members are eager to keep going. This is vital for the health and longevity of the group. The date and place of the next meeting should be confirmed.

10. It is good to follow the meeting with fifteen to twenty minutes of social time for those who are able to stay. Simple refreshments are a nice touch, with emphasis on the word simple. Otherwise people feel pressured to keep up with high expectations.

The Art of Community

Your group is a small community and, like any community, its health and vibrancy will depend on good (though not always perfect!) human relationships. That is the reason the principles of "Group Etiquette" are included on page 18 of the study guide. They should be pointed out at the first session.

Group Etiquette

- Pray for the members of your group between sessions.

- Maintain confidentiality.

- Be a good listener and encourage everyone to contribute to the discussion, without anyone monopolizing. Members that are more talkative should allow everyone a chance to respond to a discussion question before they speak a second time.

- Love your neighbor by speaking charitably and refraining from any kind of gossip.

- Be on time, come prepared, and actively take part in discussion and prayer.

- Be open and expect God's action in your life and prayer—expect to be changed!

The "Answer Prompts"

The remainder of this Facilitator's Guide consists of the discussion questions from the eight sessions of the study guide. Some of them include "answer prompts" in italics. As you know, these are not contained in the study guide itself. They are provided to you as facilitator in the event that they may be helpful, keeping in mind point number 4 in the "Keys" above.

It is natural that group members will want to know, "What does your book say?" And it is fine to tell them, as long as people have made a good effort to give their own answers first.

You will see that many of the discussion questions do not have answer prompts after them. That is the result of a judgment about which ones perhaps needed the extra support, especially for doctrinal clarity, and which ones would be best left to the group members to work through on their own.

May God bless your group's Catechism study and make it fruitful!

Christopher Ruff, S.T.L.

Session 1

A Symphony of the Faith

Reflection on
Introduction by
Pope John Paul II
and nn. 1-49

We reflect briefly on two key texts of Blessed Pope John Paul II, and then take our first step into the Catechism itself.

Discussion Questions

1. Some of us grew up with the Baltimore Catechism, which had its roots in the *Catechism of the Council of Trent* from the 16th century (the only other universal catechism in the history of the Church). Both the Baltimore Catechism and the *Catechism of the Catholic Church* contain the same fundamental truths, but the manner of expression is different.

   From the little you have seen so far of this Catechism, how would you characterize the difference, if you remember the Baltimore Catechism (if you are too young, search for it on the Internet and have a look)? Why do you suppose many say the manner of expression of this Catechism is more suited to the times in which we live?

   The Baltimore Catechism was a fruit of the U.S. Bishops' meeting at the Third Plenary Council of Baltimore in 1884. It was first published in 1885, in the form of 1400 questions and answers in 37 lessons. To help in answering this question, here is a sample from an edition published in 1891:

   1. **Q. Who made the world?** A. God made the world.

2. **Q. Who is God?** *A. God is the Creator of heaven and earth, and of all things.*

3. **Q. What is man?** *A. Man is a creature composed of body and soul, and made to the image and likeness of God.*

6. **Q. Why did God make you?** *A. God made me to know Him, to love Him, and to serve Him in this world, and to be happy with Him for ever in heaven.*

9. **9. Q. What must we do to save our souls?** *A. To save our souls, we must worship God by faith, hope, and charity; that is, we must believe in Him, hope in Him, and love Him with all our heart.*

2. In *Fidei Depositum,* the Pope writes that on every level the Church is "called to a new effort of evangelization." And the Catechism states: "Those who with God's help have welcomed Christ's call and freely responded to it are urged on by love of Christ to proclaim the Good News everywhere in the world" (n. 3). Yet Catholic lay people very often seem to be shy about evangelizing others, calling them to Christ and to faith. Why do you suppose this is? If we were less shy about it, what would we be doing, what *should* we be doing, day to day?

On Mission Sunday, January 6, 2012, Pope Benedict XVI proclaimed:

> *We...need to recover the same apostolic zeal as that of the early Christian communities....The encounter with Christ as a living Person, who satisfies the thirst of the heart [must] lead to the desire to share with others the joy of this presence and to make him known, so that all may experience this joy.... [F]aith...is the most important gift which has been made to us in our lives and which we cannot keep to ourselves.*

As to why we are shy about evangelizing others, consider this: Do we have the "apostolic zeal" Pope Benedict XVI is calling for? Have we encountered

Christ "as a living Person" through prayer, the Sacraments, spiritual reading, etc.? Do we really have a relationship with him? Or are we too often going through the motions in living our Catholic Faith? Maybe it is time for renewal! As the old saying goes, "You can't give what you don't have."

Also, have we been intimidated by the lie that faith and religion are private things that everyone should keep to themselves?

As to how we can and should evangelize, we do not need to go door to door (though some may be called to that). Daily life offers plenty of opportunities to share with others—especially when they are facing suffering or challenges—what Christ and his Church have meant to us.

3. The Prologue to the Catechism ends with a beautiful quote from the *Catechism of the Council of Trent:*

> "The whole concern of doctrine and its teaching must be directed to the love that never ends. Whether something is proposed for belief, for hope or for action, the love of our Lord must always be made accessible, so that anyone can see that all the works of perfect Christian virtue spring from love and have no other objective than to arrive at love."

What is the essential message here, and the importance of that message?

In answering this question, consider Jesus' words in the Gospel of Matthew:

> *And one of them, a lawyer, asked him a question, to test him. "Teacher, which is the great commandment in the law?" And he said to him, "You shall love the Lord your God with all your heart, and with all your soul, and with all your mind. This is the great and first commandment. And a second is like it, You shall love your neighbor as yourself. On these two commandments depend all the law and the prophets" (Mt 22:35-40).*

Reflect also on Paul's words to the Corinthians:

> *If I speak in the tongues of men and of angels, but have not love, I am a noisy gong or a clanging cymbal. And if I have prophetic powers, and understand all mysteries and all knowledge, and if I have all faith, so as to remove mountains, but have not love, I am nothing (1 Cor 13:1-2).*

4. Have someone read n. 27. Is the desire for God written in your heart? How do you know? How does it manifest itself?

5. Number 29 lists a number of factors that can bring man to forget, overlook, or even explicitly reject his bond with God. Have you seen some of these factors at work in the world? Discuss.

6. Read the quote from Pope Pius XII in n. 37. Is the point he is making evident in society today—indeed, even in our own lives at times? Discuss.

7. Numbers 31-35 and 41 note that all creation reflects God in some way, especially man, so that "from the greatness and beauty of created things comes a corresponding perception of their Creator" (Wisdom 13:5).

    What realities or characteristics in the human person and in the natural world draw you closer to an awareness of God? Can you think of a time when God became quite real and close to you because of something you saw in another person or in nature?

Session 2

God Comes to Meet Us

Reflection on
nn. 50-141

We reflect on the manner in which God has revealed himself to us, particularly through Sacred Scripture and Tradition, faithfully handed on by the Church.

Discussion Questions

1. The Catechism teaches that Jesus is the fulfillment of all God's Revelation, the final and unsurpassable Word. What attributes of God do you see revealed in the life of Christ? Point to some incidents in the Gospels that illustrate those attributes.

2. Discuss the difference between public Revelation and private revelations (see nn. 66-67). What are some examples of private revelations that have been approved by the Church?

   Public Revelation consists of:

   - *The Sacred Scriptures.*

   - *Tradition (with a capital "T"), or definitive beliefs and practices that may not be contained explicitly in Scripture, but that have been passed down to us from the age of the Apostles.*

This Public Revelation forms the deposit of faith that must be passed on in every era and that demands from us a response of faith. Public Revelation reached completion in the age of the Apostles and can never be added to (though it can be understood and articulated with greater depth with the aid of the Holy Spirit).

On the other hand, "private revelations" have occurred over the centuries, and some have been recognized as worthy of belief by the authority of the Church. "They do not belong, however, to the deposit of faith..." (n. 67). Some examples of private revelations recognized by the Church are the apparitions of Jesus and his Sacred Heart to St. Margaret Mary Alacoque in the 17th century and the apparitions of Mary as Our Lady of Guadalupe (16th century Mexico), Our Lady of Lourdes (1858, France) and Our Lady of Fatima (1917, Portugal).

3. Each of us is indebted to certain people who in the course of our lives were instrumental in encouraging and forming our faith. Who has affected your life in this way, and how?

4. We read in n. 79 that the "...Father's self-communication, made through his Word in the Holy Spirit, remains present and active in the Church: 'God, who spoke in the past, continues to converse with the Spouse of his beloved Son' *(Dei Verbum, 8)*."

    In other words, God continues to act in the Church and to communicate himself through her.

    It is obvious in today's world that there is a crisis of faith on precisely this point. Many (including many Catholics) do not believe Christ's words, "He who hears you, hears me" (Luke 10:16), with reference to the Church.

    - What influences have fostered this doubt?

    - What can we do to help preserve in ourselves and our loved ones a vibrant faith that to hear the Church is to hear Christ?

5. Define each of the following and describe how they are related to one another:

   a) Scripture;
   b) Tradition;
   c) Magisterium.

a) Scripture is the inspired word of God contained in the 46 books of the Old Testament and the 27 books of the New.

b) Tradition refers to what the apostles handed on— orally and by their actions and decisions—from all that they "received from Jesus' teaching and example and what they learned from the Holy Spirit" (n. 83). This includes elements that are not absolutely explicit in the Bible, such as the basic form of the Mass (see n. 1345), the precise number of the Sacraments, the manner in which successors to the apostles (the bishops) would be ordained, the practice of offering Masses for the dead, etc.

Even our most central belief in God as a Trinity of Persons in one God, though it is clearly grounded in the Bible, was shaped in important ways by Church Tradition under the guidance of the Holy Spirit. The early Councils of the Church professed, for example, that all three Persons of the Trinity are coeternal and "consubstantial" ("of one substance"). They professed that the Father generates the Son from all eternity and that the Holy Spirit proceeds from the

Father and the Son. None of this is unequivocally clear from Scripture alone, but it can be known with certainty through the workings of the Holy Spirit in Church Tradition.

c) The Magisterium consists of the Pope and the bishops in communion with him in their teaching authority (magister is Latin for "teacher") over the entire Church.

*How are these related? As the Catechism says, "Sacred Tradition and Sacred Scripture are bound closely together" and both "flow out of the same divine well-spring" (n. 80). As Catholics, we do not focus exclusively on Scripture, detaching it from Tradition. Indeed, "the first generation of Christians **did not yet have a written New Testament, and the New Testament itself demonstrates the process of living Tradition"** (n. 83).*

*In other words, the writings of the New Testament are for all intents and purposes a divinely inspired record of what the Tradition was already saying and doing. Not only that, but it was Church Tradition that settled, once and for all, which books were part of that inspired record and thus **belonged** to the Bible.*

Finally, it is the Magisterium of the Church that, acting as the successors of Peter and the Apostles, has been charged by Christ with the responsibility of passing on and interpreting the deposit of faith (made up of Scripture and Tradition) for every age.

6. Read together nn. 91-93 of the Catechism, with regard to the *sensus fidei.* How can we understand this in light of the fact that substantial numbers of people who call themselves Catholic actively disagree with the Magisterium (Pope and bishops) on key teachings, especially in the area of morality?

The sensus fidei, or "supernatural appreciation of faith," is a gift of the Holy Spirit given to the faithful as a whole, just as the Catechism states. It does not, however, follow that everyone who calls himself Catholic will have an active share in this gift. If one stands opposed to the teaching authority of the Church on certain matters, this can block the action of the Holy Spirit, and in that position one can certainly hold erroneous judgments.

*But it is precisely the body of the **faithful**—those who trust that in hearing the Church they hear Christ (cf. Lk 10:16)—that, "aroused and sustained by the Spirit of truth" and "guided by the sacred teaching authority (Magisterium)....unfailingly adheres to this faith, penetrates it more deeply with right judgment, and applies it more fully in daily life" (n. 93).*

7. Numbers 115-119 of the Catechism discuss two fundamental meanings of Scripture: the literal sense and the spiritual sense.

    Read Exodus 12:1-13. What is this "literally" about? What is its spiritual sense (specifically "allegorical" —see n. 117 of the Catechism)? It may help you also to read John 1:29, Luke 22:14-20 and Revelation 5:6-14 to get the full impact of the spiritual/allegorical sense.

    Exodus 12:1-13 is literally about God's prescription of the Passover meal / sacrifice and the way that the first-born among the Israelites would be spared death by the blood of the Passover lamb sprinkled on the lintel and the doorposts.

    In its spiritual / allegorical sense, this passage foreshadows Christ as the true Passover lamb, whose blood would save us all from the death of sin and lead us to the Promised Land of Heaven.

8. In discussing the unique place of the four Gospels in the Church's life, the Catechism quotes St. Therese of Lisieux:

> "But above all it's the Gospels that occupy my mind when I'm at prayer; my poor soul has so many needs, and yet this is the one thing needful. I'm always finding fresh lights there, hidden and enthralling meanings" (*Autobiography,* Manuscript A).

- What parts of the Bible have spoken to you most profoundly?

- Do you have a favorite Gospel or Gospel passage?

- What helps you or hinders you in making the Bible a significant part of your life of personal prayer and devotion?

Session 3

Our Response of Faith

Reflection on
nn. 142-197

*We reflect on our proper response, stirred
by the Holy Spirit, to God who has revealed
himself.*

Discussion Questions

1. The Catechism tells us that faith is a gift of God and that man's heart must be stirred and converted by the Holy Spirit, "who opens the eyes of the mind and 'makes it easy for all to accept and believe the truth'" (n. 153). But the Catechism adds that God has wished to aid our faith by providing *external proofs* of his Revelation, including "the miracles of Christ and the saints, prophecies, the Church's growth and holiness, and her fruitfulness and stability" (n. 156).

   - Which of these "external proofs" of God's Revelation have bolstered your faith?
   - Are there any other external supports that have helped you?

2. The Catechism in n. 158 quotes a famous saying of St. Augustine: "I believe, in order to understand; and I understand, the better to believe" *(Sermo 43,7,9)*. What do you think he meant by this rather mysterious phrase?

We can break it into its two parts:

a) "I believe, in order to understand":

Belief, or faith, facilitates understanding because it opens us to the grace of the Holy Spirit, who has been sent, as Jesus said, to "lead you into all truth" (Jn 16:13).

In short, the more you commit yourself to the truths of the Faith, the more you will be led by the Spirit who gives understanding. This kind of understanding does not have its ultimate source in books, and that is why it is often some of the simplest people who possess it. Remember Jesus' words: "I thank thee, Father, Lord of heaven and earth, that thou hast hidden these things from the wise and understanding and revealed them to babes" (Mt 11:25).

b) "I understand, the better to believe":

Augustine is saying here that he does not explore the truths of the Faith out of intellectual curiosity or pride. He reads and studies and meditates with only one end in view—he wishes his mind to penetrate the truths of the Faith more deeply so that he may embrace them more fully.

And so the circle is complete—deeper faith leads to deeper understanding, which then leads to an even deeper faith, and round and round it goes.

3. We read in n. 161 that belief in Jesus Christ and in the One who sent him is necessary for salvation. What about those who—especially in the past, but even today—have never heard of Christ? Look ahead to nn. 846-848 and discuss.

*From reading nn. 846-848 it should be clear that God will judge each of us based on what we have done with what we **know**. Even if we are never taught anything explicit about God or his Gospel, he still speaks to each of us through the laws he has written in human conscience. To those who listen to his voice in their consciences and seek to live according to it, God, in ways unknown to us, can grant grace and salvation. But even in such a case, the gift of grace and salvation comes only through Christ and his Body the Church, because there is no other source and channel of grace, whether the recipient is aware of it or not.*

4. In n. 162, the Catechism connects certain conditions with either perseverance in, or the loss of, the gift of faith. Discuss one by one these conditions and the relevance you think each has to faith.

5. The Catechism is not naive about the challenge of faith, quoting St. Paul's words in n. 164, that we perceive God as "in a mirror, dimly" and only "in part" (1 Cor 13:12). It notes that faith is often tested by the world we live in, by the realities of evil, suffering, injustice and death. These can shake us and tempt us to lose faith.

   • What do you see as the greatest challenges to faith? What has helped you to deal with them?

   • Why do you suppose God has not made everything crystal clear and easy? Read 1 Peter 1:3-9 for insight.

In answer to the second question, the confusion and difficulty man experiences is the result of original sin and his own personal sin, and God certainly cannot be blamed for that. In respecting our freedom, God has permitted this state of affairs. But the good news is that these painful challenges present us with an opportunity to be put to the test, to be tried "like gold in the fire"(cf.,1 Pt 1:7), so that we may grow stronger in following God out of real conviction and steadfastness and love.

6. In n. 166, the Catechism makes a beautiful state-
    ment about the community dimension of faith,
    about our interconnectedness and reliance on one
    another. Read it together now. Do you sense the
    truth of this statement? When and how has it be-
    come real for you?

7. Some would say that in today's world many people have a reawakened hunger for faith, for certainties, for sure moral teaching, and that the Catholic Church stands out for not having compromised and watered down her teachings. Discuss.

8. Pray (slowly and deliberately) the Nicene Creed together as written following n. 184. We pray it every Sunday at Mass and it links us with nearly 1700 years of Christian faith and worship. Take a moment silently to reflect on the millions of voices that have proclaimed and even died for that faith.

Session 4

The God in Whom We Believe

Reflection on
nn. 185-267

We continue to reflect on the first line of the Apostles' Creed: "I believe in God, the Father Almighty, Creator of Heaven and Earth," focusing on the central mystery of Three Persons in One God.

Discussion Questions

1. Why do you suppose God, in his revelation to the Israelites, focused so intently on his being one God and did not communicate the truth that he is also three persons?"

   Polytheism, or a belief in many gods, was the prevailing religious view in most civilizations in Old Testament times. In light of these dominant influences, evidently God saw that the Israelites needed first to consolidate a belief in **one** *God over all creation. Otherwise they might easily have seen the Trinity as three separate gods, failing to come to grips with the unity of the three persons.*

2. In n. 206, the Catechism says that in telling Moses he was YHWH (Yahweh), God in one sense revealed a name, but in another sense *refused* to accept a name.

    *   Read the paragraph in question and discuss what you think the Catechism means by this.

    *   Mention two or three other insights that made an impression on you from this section on the significance of God's "name" (nn. 203-213).

We see in n. 206 that "Yahweh" means "I AM HE WHO IS," "I AM WHO AM" or "I AM WHO I AM." That is indeed a certain revelation of God's identity, because it reveals him as the God who is always there, who lives outside time in an eternal present, an eternal NOW.

At the same time, God seems to be answering Moses' question, "What is your name?" by saying, in effect: "Don't try to give me a name—I am beyond names, I am indescribable, I simply AM WHO I AM."

3. Number 208 states, "Faced with God's fascinating and mysterious presence, man discovers his own insignificance." The Catechism then gives examples from the Bible in which men such as Isaiah in the Old Testament and Peter in the New Testament shrink from God's awesome presence out of a sense of their own unworthiness.

    *   Do you think we have sometimes lost a sense of this "fear of the Lord" in recent decades, and if so, why?

    *   Might it have been a reaction to something else?

It seems we have lived through several decades that have focused on being "comfortable" with ourselves —"I'm okay, you're okay." That spirit of self-satisfaction naturally feels threatened by a God overwhelming in his holiness and grandeur, a God who calls us continually to humble conversion.

It can be argued, though, that the "I'm okay" trend was triggered to some degree by a way of presenting God that was too severe and frightening, that showed him too much as Judge and too little as the Father of Mercies. The correct balance is well illustrated in nn. 208, 210 and 211.

4. Read Jesus' dialogue with the Jews in the Gospel of John 8:39-59. Discuss the profound significance of Jesus' choice of words in verse 58 (see n. 211).

In saying, "Before Abraham was, I AM," Jesus does two things:

- *He adopts the same name Yahweh had revealed to Moses, thus pointing to his divine nature;*

- *He implies that his existence is not bound by time with its past, present and future. In his divine nature as the Son, the second Person of the Trinity, he lives in an eternal NOW.*

5. Read the beautiful prayer of St. Teresa of Jesus in n. 227.

  • What difference do you think a prayer like that might make if you started and ended your day with it?

  • If there are any particular prayers that inspire and strengthen your faith, mention them and discuss why.

6. The main points of the Church's doctrine on the Trinity are discussed in the Catechism (nn. 232-267) and in the commentary for this session.

   - In reading about this great and central mystery of three persons in one God, were there particular aspects that were clarified or reinforced for you? Discuss.

   - You may better acquaint yourselves with some of the roots of this doctrine in the New Testament by reading together from the Gospel of John 14:1-26; 15:26-27; 16:12-15; 16:25-28 and 17:1-5.

Session 5

The Father Almighty

Reflection on
nn. 268-354

We continue to reflect on the first line of the Apostles' Creed: "I believe in God, the Father Almighty, Creator of Heaven and Earth," now turning our attention to the wonder of creation.

Discussion Questions

1. Number 269 affirms our belief in God as the "master of history." If indeed nothing can thwart God's design, his plans, does that mean we are simply actors reciting our predetermined lines in a play written by God? In other words, how can we as Catholics defend our belief in free will in light of our belief in God as master of history?

*God is the master of history without negating our free will. One of the keys here is that God exists outside time. For him, there is no "before" or "after." There is only one eternal "now." So God, in his divine wisdom, power and love, is able to weave together all the **freely chosen** actions of mankind's past, present and future in one ultimate design. The evil actions and consequences are woven together with the good actions and consequences in such a way that the good ultimately triumphs. For example, the death of a martyr is evil on the part of the executioner but good on the part of the one who gives his life for Christ, and this good far outshines the evil.*

We must be careful not to minimize pain and suffering, or the horror of real evil, for we recall that even Jesus wept over Jerusalem (Lk 19:41) and at the tomb of Lazarus (Jn 11:35) and sweated blood as he contemplated the Passion he would undergo (Lk 22:44). Yet we know that God is greater than evil and always has the last word. How exactly God works this out remains a mystery well beyond our grasp, but it is a core conviction of our faith that he does. In the words of St. Paul, "We know that in everything God works for good with those who love him" (Rom 8:28). And remember, St. Paul was beheaded for his faith in Christ.

The greatest example of good being drawn from evil —far surpassing all others—is the death of Christ on the cross, by which the powers of evil were decisively defeated.

2. What does the Catechism state is God's greatest display of power (n. 270)? In what moment of Christ's life was it made most evident (n. 272)?

3. Toward the end of World War II, British Prime Minister Winston Churchill cautioned Russian dicctator Joseph Stalin to respect the Catholic Church. Stalin scornfully replied, "How many divisions does the Pope of Rome have?" Stalin understood power only as brute force, and the power of Communism seemed unstoppable for decades. But his question was answered in 1989 when the Berlin Wall came tumbling down and Eastern Europe emerged from Communist oppression thanks largely to the influence of Pope John Paul II (along with the unseen power of prayer).

What do we learn from examples like this about the various faces of "power?" From the point of view of the Gospel, name a few of the most powerful men and women in history and describe why and how they were powerful.

4. In number 305 we read: "Jesus asks for childlike abandonment to the providence of our heavenly Father who takes care of his children's smallest needs..."

    - Why is this attitude of "childlike abandonment" not easy for us?
    - What is helpful in fostering it? What gets in the way?

5. In nn. 309-314 the Catechism treats the mystery of the existence of evil in a world created and governed by an all-good, all-powerful God. This mystery has troubled many minds and hearts throughout history. Indeed, evil and the suffering it brings are painfully present to all of us. As you read this section, make note of any phrases or ideas that you find especially helpful in grappling with this mystery. Discuss.

6. The Catechism offers us a beautiful reflection on the nature and mission of the angels in nn. 331-336.

    • Discuss what stood out for you from this section.

    • How much thought have you given to the fact that you have a guardian angel?

    • Did you learn the classic prayer to your guardian angel? Probably many people think of it as just a prayer for children to say. What do you think? Pray it together and discuss the kinds of guidance and protection you think God intends your guardian angel to give you:

Prayer to Guardian Angel:

> "Angel of God, my guardian dear, to whom God's love commits me here, ever this day (night) be at my side, to light and guard, to rule and guide. Amen."

Our guardian angels are first of all meant to assist us in doing good, resisting evil and getting to heaven, and we should explicitly ask their help in this. They can also provide physical protection and help, and there are many accounts of them suddenly appearing and doing just that, some of which have been described in books and even secular news reports. Saints like St. Padre Pio, St. Rose of Lima and St. Gemma Galgani—and many others—frequently saw and conversed with their guardian angels, treasuring their holy companionship and help.

*We just need to remember that the angels' role is always to point the way to Christ through his Church, because, as the Catechism tells us, "Christ is the center of the angelic world" (n. 331). Those who want angels **without** Christ, as in "spirit guides" in some New Age cults, may end up caught in the web of fallen angels in disguise.*

7. In nn. 339-349 we are given the principles for what
   we could call a Catholic ecology, or respect for the
   created world God has placed us in, with its living
   creatures and natural resources.

   List some of these principles, putting them in your
   own words, and discuss them in the group. How
   would you compare this model of ecology with the
   more secular model?

   A partial list of principles includes:

   - *There is a hierarchy in visible creation,
     with man at the top. This means that while
     we must show due respect for the goodness
     of the created world (refraining from cru-
     elty and senseless destruction), plants and
     animals do not have "rights" of the kind
     humans have. They are subordinate to our
     needs (for food, etc.).*

   - *There is an interdependence of all creatures
     that we must not be reckless about.*

   - *There is beauty in the world God has given
     us which we should admire and for which
     we should praise God.*

Sometimes the secular model of ecology loses a sense of due proportion and hierarchy. It is then that one sees people advocating for "the right to choose" to kill baby humans by abortion but obsessed with saving baby whales or spotted owls. When God and his revelation are out of the picture, there is the danger of making a distorted ecology into a kind of god.

Session 6

The Mystery of Man

Reflection on
nn. 355-421

We continue to reflect on the first line of the Apostles' Creed—"I believe in God, the Father Almighty, Creator of Heaven and Earth"—now focusing on the creation, fall and redemption of man.

Discussion Questions

1. Much of this session focuses on man's fall, on original sin. But in spite of the tragic reality of sin, the Christian message remains one of joy and beauty.

    As a way of reaffirming this, have someone read aloud the two quotes in small print in nn. 356 and 358.

    What particularly strikes you from these quotes, and why?

2. As Catholics we hold that the human person is a unity of body and soul. We even say that after death we are incomplete until our soul is reunited with our glorified body at the final Resurrection.

    Some other philosophies and religious traditions have held the body to be the prison of the soul, from which the soul must be liberated.

    Why do you think some people would be tempted to see the body in this latter, negative way? What would you point to in Sacred Scripture, in the Catechism, and in your own experience, that supports the Christian view of the goodness of the body?

    Why do some see the body negatively? As a consequence of original sin, clearly this earthly body of ours is subject to fatigue, pain, sickness and death. Also, many temptations to excess are connected with the body: alcohol and drug abuse, gluttony, lust, etc. In so many ways the body can seem to weigh us down, and because of this there can be the wish to soar free from the body.

    But Scripture tells us that when God created the visible world he "saw that it was good" (cf., Gen 1). And the Son of God united a human nature, with a body, to his divine nature. There can be no greater evidence of the goodness of bodily existence than that. Christ rose from the dead and thus brought the body into divine glory. Christ will have his risen body for all eternity and the bodies of the just who rejoice with him in heaven will also be glorified. Never again will they feel pain or weariness, but only radiant wellbeing and joy.

For more evidence of the goodness of the body, read the small print in n. 364.

3. Imagine yourself suddenly transported back in time before the fall, before original sin. List the ways in which life would be different (see nn. 374-378). But would something be missing (see n. 412)?

Our friendship with God would be unbroken. There would be no sickness, suffering or death, nor even the pains of childbirth. Our minds and wills would be clear and strong, and our human emotions and urges would be in harmony rather than pulling us in unhealthy and/or sinful directions. Our families would be harmonious. Husbands and wives would never argue. Teenagers wouldn't rebel. Work would always be a joyful, fulfilling form of expression.

What would be missing would be the God-Man Jesus Christ as merciful Redeemer, since in our sinless state we would not need redemption. The Son of God, Second Person of the Trinity, would not have needed to take on our human nature to die and rise for us. The Church tells us that in spite of the effects of original sin we are at a more "exalted" level now than Adam and Eve were, because through Baptism we are joined to Christ.

But of course we also struggle with ills that were not part of Paradise, especially our sinful inclinations. But on balance we are better off, says the Church. That is why we can can sing in the Exultet, "Oh happy fault... which gained for us so great a Redeemer" (cf., n. 412).

This does not mean to exclude the possibility that Christ could have incarnated even without our needing redemption, but that is a matter of pure speculation.

4. Read numbers 386 and 387. When human persons and societies reject the notion of original sin and personal sin, when they fail to see man as fallen and inclined to sin, what consequences follow? And what attitude does that foster toward Christ's suffering and death for us (see n. 389)?

The rejection of the idea that man is fallen and inclined to sin leads to the belief that human problems are all the result of psychological conflicts or external, societal pressures, etc. People then fail to see the need for repentance and conversion of heart. They rationalize their misbehavior. We see, too, the tendency to believe that every social problem has a political rather than a moral or spiritual solution.

Finally, if we believe we are not fallen, not stained by sin, then we dismiss the notion that we need mercy or redemption. So a kind of rejection of, or indifference toward, Christ's sufferings is fostered.

5. Number 397 says of original sin that "Man, tempted by the devil, let his trust in his Creator die in his heart and, abusing his freedom, disobeyed God's command.... All subsequent sin would be disobedience toward God and lack of trust in his goodness."

The disobedience part is easy to see, but how does sin reflect a lack of trust in God's goodness (see Genesis 3:1-11)?

In Genesis 3:1-11, Satan paints a picture of God as lying and jealous. "You will not die" if you eat of the tree of the knowledge of good and evil, the serpent tells Eve. In fact, "God knows that when you eat of it your eyes will be opened, and you will be like God" (Gen. 3:4-5).

The impression given is that God is jealously keeping us from some fulfillment, some happiness that we ought to have. That is what we mean by a lack of trust in God's goodness. So sin is not only disobedience, but the ridiculous notion that there is a better way to happiness than God's way, and the belief that he wants to keep us from it.

6. We see from n. 406 that the Church's teaching about original sin and man's fallen nature walks a middle course between the opposite extremes of Pelagius on the one hand and the first Protestant reformers on the other. In your own words, say how this is so.

In brief, Pelagianism says that original sin is not an inherited state, but just bad example. Thus we don't need God's cleansing grace to be relieved of it. We just need to choose not to follow Adam and Eve's bad example, and we can do that under our own strength.

The Protestant reformers, on the other hand, claimed that original sin totally corrupted our natures, so that we can do nothing good.

The Catholic Church teaches that original sin is truly an inherited state from which we must be cleansed by the grace of God through baptism, but that our natures are not totally corrupted, only weakened. We can thus freely do some humanly good things without grace, but to perform supernaturally meritorious actions, we must be motivated by a love that can only come to us as a grace from God.

In short, we're neither as pure as Pelagius believed nor as corrupted and enslaved as the reformers believed. But we do need grace for salvation.

Session 7

And the Word Became Flesh

Reflection on
nn. 422-483

We begin our reflection on the Creed's statement of faith: "I Believe in Jesus Christ, the Only Son of God."

Discussion Questions

1. Let someone in the group read 1 John 1:1-4, quoted
    in nn. 425. After a silent pause for reflection, dis-
    cuss what especially strikes you from this passage.

2. N. 428 states: "Whoever is called 'to teach Christ' must first seek 'the surpassing worth of knowing Christ Jesus'...."

Have you ever heard Christ preached or spoken of in such a way that your heart stirred and you felt inside, "This person knows Christ, intimately"?

- What was it that made you feel that way?
- How do you think a person arrives at that degree of "knowing" Christ?
- What helps, and what gets in the way?

3. Read the accounts of Jesus' baptism in Luke 3:21-22
    and John 1:31-34. How was Jesus' "eternal messi-
    anic consecration" revealed at that event?

    *Through the Holy Spirit descending in the form of
    a dove, and the Father's voice from heaven—"Thou
    art my beloved Son; with thee I am well pleased" (Lk
    3:22).*

4. In n. 440, the Catechism speaks of two dimensions of Christ's messianic kingship that must always be borne in mind together. What are they? (Hint: Peter was inclined to look for only one dimension—and to be repulsed and scandalized by the other).

The two dimensions are:

- *Jesus' transcendent identity, his glory as the Son of Man who "came down from heaven"(cf., Jn 6:33) and who will return in glory "on the clouds"(cf., Mk 13:26) coming in judgment;*

- *Jesus' identity as the "Suffering Servant" who came "not to be served but to serve, and to give his life as a ransom for many"(Mk 10:45).*

Peter was enthused about the first dimension (see Mt 17:1-4), but horrified by the second (see Mt 16:21-25).

5. What especially struck you from the reflection on
    the four names or titles of Jesus in nn. 430-451?

6. At the end of a discussion of Jesus as "Lord" (nn. 446-451), we see quoted what is nearly the last line of the Bible, the heartfelt cry, "Come, Lord Jesus!" (Revelation 22:20). That cry should echo in the heart of every Christian and every parish community.

Are there particular prayers, devotions or images that help keep that cry alive in your heart? Are there liturgical or devotional moments or seasons in which that cry seems to come alive in your parish in a particular way?

7. Discuss the four reasons the Word became flesh for us (see nn. 457-460).

    The four reasons are:

    a. *to save us by reconciling us with God*
    b. *so that we might know God's love*
    c. *to be our model of holiness*
    d. *to make us partakers of the divine nature*

8. To what temptation did Adam and Eve succumb (see Genesis 3:4)? How did Jesus precisely reverse that sin (see the quote from St. Paul in n. 461)?

Adam and Eve succumbed to the proud temptation to be "like God," though they were mere humans created by God. Jesus reverses that sin because he who is truly God "did not count equality with God a thing to be grasped, but emptied himself, taking the form of a servant." He "humbled himself and became obedient" (Philippians 2:5-8).

9. Share together your understanding of the manner in which Christ has two natures in one Person. When all is said and done, of course, this is one of the deepest mysteries of our Faith.

   See this session's summary, as well as the text of the Catechism.

Session 8

Jesus' Birth and Public Ministry

Reflection on
nn. 484-570

We continue our reflection on "Jesus Christ, the Only Son of God," turning our attention to the Virgin Mary and to the mysteries of the life of Christ from his birth through his public ministry.

Discussion Questions

1. Sometimes Catholics are accused of worshiping Mary, treating her virtually as Christ's equal. What would you point to in this section of the Catechism to show that this is not the case—that in fact Mary is kept in the proper perspective (see, for example, nn. 487, 492, 494)?

2. The Church teaches that Mary was a virgin not only in the conception and birth of Jesus, but throughout the rest of her life (she was "ever virgin"). In seeking to understand the significance of this virginity, which of the points in nn. 502-507 strike you as most helpful, and why?

See the text of the Catechism. Another point that could be offered is the following:

> *Some say that the teaching on Mary's continued virginity is a way of devaluing human sexuality, of saying that sexual relations, even in marriage, are somehow "impure." But this is not at all the intent of that teaching.*

An analogy may help to clarify this:

> *No one would say there is anything wrong with enjoying a picnic lunch with family and friends—indeed, that sort of fellowship is a wonderful and precious part of life. But you would never spread out a picnic lunch on the altar where the Eucharist is celebrated! The altar is consecrated exclusively for one sacred meal— the Eucharistic banquet. In the same way, even though human sexuality in marriage has great value and dignity, in Mary's case there was a special consecration of the womb for the Son of God and no other.*

3. In discussing the "mysteries" of Christ's life, n. 515 states: "From the swaddling clothes of his birth to the vinegar of his Passion and the shroud of his Resurrection, everything in Jesus' life was a sign of his mystery." Discuss the deeper meaning or sign value of the following facts:

    - At Jesus' birth he was laid in a manger, which is a feeding trough.

    - Jesus lived a hidden and obedient life in a town of no importance for 30 years.

    - It was Mary's intercession that prompted Jesus to work his first miracle at Cana.

    - When a paralytic was lowered through a roof for healing, Jesus first forgave his sins before healing him physically.

    - Jesus' sacrificial death took place at the time of Passover.

    - Jesus' risen and glorified body continued to show the wounds of his Passion.

    Let each person in your group try to think of one other incident or fact of Jesus' life that is a sign pointing to a deeper meaning.

The deeper meaning or sign value of these facts is, respectively:

- *Jesus is our food, the Bread from Heaven, the Eucharist.*

- *Jesus' hidden life is a sign of the goodness and holiness of "ordinary life" when it is lived in the proper spirit.*

- *The miracle at Cana is a sign of the great intercessory power of Mary.*

- *Jesus' mission is first of all to redeem souls, with ministry to our bodies secondary.*

- *Jesus is the new Passover Lamb, whose blood saves us from slavery to sin (as the first Passover lamb saved the Israelites from slavery in Egypt).*

- *The wounds of Christ's death are not signs of defeat and death, but signs of love, glory and new life won by the Cross—the "tree of death" is the "tree of life."*

83

4. What are the 10 mysteries of the Rosary that medi-
    tate on the birth, infancy and public life of Jesus
    (recall that Pope John Paul II added the Luminous
    Mysteries)? What are a few points discussed in this
    section of the Catechism that might give you more
    food for meditation when you pray the mysteries of
    the Rosary?

    *Joyful Mysteries: Annunciation of Angel Gabriel to
    Mary; Visitation of Mary to Elizabeth; Birth of
    Jesus; Presentation in the Temple; Finding of the
    Child Jesus in the Temple*

    *Luminous Mysteries: Baptism of Jesus; Miracle at
    the Wedding Feast of Cana; Proclamation of the
    Kingdom; Transfiguration; Institution of the Eucha-
    rist*

5. We read in n. 521 that "Christ enables us *to live in him* all that he himself lived, and *he lives it in us.*" What is the meaning of this statement (read the rest of 521 for help)? What might be a concrete example of it taking place in a person's life?

Everything in the life of Christ points to love, obedience, humility, meekness, self-sacrifice, zeal for souls, poverty, etc. We must transpose into our own lives the spirit that washed feet; that touched always to heal, never to harm; that in every decision looked first to the will of the Father; that always found time for prayer; that suffered patiently and in love.

Example: An elderly person incapacitated in a nursing home can live out the mystery of suffering in union with Christ.

6. In n. 548 we are told of the many ways people re-
    acted to the miracles of Christ. Go through each of
    these ways of responding and consider how they can
    be applicable to people today, whether in regard to
    Christ's miracles or in regard to signs and miracles
    worked by God in more modern times (such as the
    miracles worked through St. Padre Pio, the heal-
    ings of Lourdes, or maybe something extraordinary
    that has touched you or someone you know).

7. In nn. 554-556, we read of Jesus' Transfiguration
    and how closely it was linked to his prediction of
    his Passion and death (See Matthew 17:1-13). What
    was the lesson Peter and the others needed to learn
    —and that we must learn—from this linkage (see
    the small print in nn. 555 and 556)?

*There is no glory without the loving sacrifice of the
cross. We cannot "pitch a tent" in the radiant glory
of the mountaintop until we have shared lovingly in
the Cross of Calvary.*

The Discipleship Series

Novo Millennio Press